T0195839

"Tanner and the Not-So-Little Fib"

Scarlett R. Smith

WestBow Press books may be ordered through booksellers or by contacting:

WestBow Press
A Division of Thomas Nelson & Zondervan
1663 Liberty Drive
Bloomington, IN 47403
www.westbowpress.com
844-714-3454

Scripture taken from the American Standard Version of the Bible.

ISBN: 978-1-6642-6530-1 (sc)
ISBN: 978-1-6642-6531-8 (e)

Library of Congress Control Number: 2022908000

Print information available on the last page.

WestBow Press rev. date: 05/17/2022

WESTBOW
PRESS®
A DIVISION OF THOMAS NELSON
& ZONDERVAN

Hi my name is Tanner. Some people call me T. My family calls me Bub. My cousin Gunner is my best bud! Him and I do a lot together, sometimes a lot of stuff that gets us into a little bit of trouble. But boy do we have a blast! One night him and I spent the night out by his pond. As we were thinking up things to do, our thinking was drowned out by the sound of bullfrogs. Slowly we turned and looked at each other as if to say, "Are you thinking what I'm thinking?" "Let's go gigging!", we hollered. OH, and by the way, It's not for the weak at heart. After a few hours, and without going into too much detail, let's just say we "hit" the jackpot! We were so excited as we tallied up our frogs! We built us a fire, cooked us up some supper, and with full tummies, we hit the sack.

It wasn't till that next evening that Gunner's mom stepped out onto their porch and noticed that something was not quite right. From the porch steps she bellowed, "Gunner! Tanner Bug! Oh, I forgot to mention, his mom calls me Tanner Bug. Having no idea, we ran up to the house to see what she wanted. Then in a very strained tone of voice, she asked, "Boys, why am I not hearing my bullfrogs?"

Quickly I responded as convincingly as I could, "We ran them out of the pond". "You ran them out of the pond?" she asked skeptically. "And just how did you do that"? "We slapped the water with our walking sticks and they hopped right out" I answered. "They just hopped right out?" she asked. "Yep, just like that", Gunner added. As she walked back in the house, she demanded, "Well you can just run them right back in!"

"Gulp", double "gulp" .... "Sure, thing mom, no problem" Gunner said.

"Oh no, what a mess we've gotten ourselves into" Gunner said in a worried tone. Tapping my chin, I reassured him, "It's just a little fib, we'll figure something out".

As we walked towards the pond, Gunner asked, "What do we do now?" I remained quiet for a while but knew there would be a solution. Finding our way to the edge of the dock we sat down, swinging our feet, skimming the top of the water. All of the sudden, I had it! "I have great idea!" I said. We will get a bucket and a net and go to my neighbor's pond and catch HIS frogs and dump them in YOUR pond!" "Excellent idea!" Gunner yelled. "We will have to tell your mom to give us a little time though", I explained. "No problem, leave that to me" Gunner reassured me.

That next morning my mom picked me up to go home And, like usual, I asked if Gunner could come with us and hang out for the day. Of course, my mom didn't mind, she loves Gunner and together we stay out of her way. We pulled in our driveway, jumped out of the car, and bolted to the barn. "I'll grab the bucket; you grab the net!" I yelled. And off to the neighbor's pond we headed. We nonchalantly ventured to the back of our garden and took a sharp right over the hill to fetch our frogs.

We quietly snuck up to the edge of the water and scooped up the bullfrogs one at a time. After what seemed to be hours, our bucket was almost too heavy for even both of us to carry. Off to the barn we scrambled with the net across the top to keep them from hopping out. Struggling up the hill, passing our garden and back into the barn, we dropped our bucket, and plopped down on a bale of hay to catch our breath.

"Now, how do we get them into the van, Gunner asked?" "That's easy. We'll put a board across the bucket and we'll load it into the back of the van before mom can notice". I exclaimed. As we loaded the bucket of frogs, I wondered how to convince mom that we needed to go BACK to Gunner's house. "I got it!" "Let's ask my mom if you can spend the night and tell her we have to go back and pick up your clothes", I explained. "You're a genius!" Gunner declared.

Grinning from ear to ear, and after persuading my mom, we headed back to his house, frogs in "hand". Pulling up to Gunner's house, my mom waited for us to jump out and retrieve his clothes. "Uh, mom," I said "why don't you go in and talk to his mom for a minute?", I insisted."Well, ok, I guess I have a few minutes, but you boys hurry up, I have to get home to cook dinner" mom said. Mom scurried up onto the porch as Gunner and I crept around to the back of the van and unloaded the frogs. Together we shuffled to the pond, keeping in step with each other so we wouldn't dump the "goods".

As we got to the water's edge, we tipped the bucket, and the frogs shot out like fireworks! "Whew!" With a sigh of relief, and engraved with big smiles, we both muttered " We did it!"

We ran up to the house and up to Gunners room to pack his bag, then back to our house we went and up to my room we ran, slamming the door behind us. "Wow" "what a job that was! I declared. That little fib wasn't so little, it turned into a lot of work" Gunner whispered. "Yeah, telling the truth would have been much easier", I said. We both agreed we would never do that again!

Mom started supper since dad would be getting home soon. As we kicked back on my bed reliving the events of the last two days, I heard a familiar voice come through the back door. There was an exchange of conversation and then all the sudden, my mom yelled up, "Bub, did you boys take all the frogs from the neighbor's pond?!"

Gunner and I quickly turned to each other, with eyebrows raised, "Oh no, not again?!"

"Whoever can be trusted with very little can also be trusted with much, and whoever is dishonest with very little will also be dishonest with much" Luke 16:10

Printed in the United States
by Baker & Taylor Publisher Services